The Conflict Resolution Library™

Dealing with Fighting
Qué hacer con las peleas

Marianne Johnston

Traducción al español:
Mauricio Velázquez de León

PowerKiDS press & Editorial Buenas Letras™
New York

Published in 2008 by The Rosen Publishing Group, Inc.
29 East 21st Street, New York, NY 10010

First Bilingual Edition

Book Design: Lissette González

Photo Credits: Cover photo © Simon Watson/Getty Images; p. 8 Shutterstock.com; p.12 by Maria Moreno; p.20 © www.istockphoto.com/Karen Struthers; all other photos by Thomas Mangieri.

Cataloging Data

Johnston, Marianne.
   Marianne Johnston / Dealing with fighting; traducción al español: Mauricio Velázquez de León.
   p. cm. – (Conflict Resolution Library/Biblioteca solución de conflictos)
Includes index.
   ISBN-13: 978-1-4042-7660-4 (library binding)
   ISBN-10: 1-4042-7660-2 (library binding)
1. Fighting–Juvenile literature. [1. Fighting. 2. Spanish language materials.] I. Title. II. Series.

Manufactured in the United States of America

Contents

Contenido

Sometimes we have **arguments** with people. When people argue, each person tries to make the other person see their side of things. When we argue we may get angry. Sometimes when we get angry we start to fight.

Algunas veces tenemos **discusiones** con los demás. Cuando discutimos, tratamos de hacer que la otra persona entienda nuestro punto de vista. Cuando discutimos, podemos enojarnos. A veces, peleamos cuando nos enojamos.

Sometimes arguments turn into verbal fights. People scream and yell at each other when they fight verbally. That doesn't do much good. The problem doesn't get solved, and both sides become even more upset.

Algunas veces, las discusiones se convierten en peleas verbales. Las personas se gritan cuando pelean verbalmente. Gritar no sirve de mucho. El problema no se resuelve, y ambas partes se enojan aun más.

A verbal fight can turn into a **physical** fight. People fight physically when they don't know how to express their feelings in words. The only thing that can come of this kind of fighting is that someone will get hurt.

Una pelea verbal puede convertirse en una pelea **física**. Peleamos físicamente cuando no sabemos expresar nuestros sentimientos con palabras. Lo único que pasa con este tipo de peleas es que alguien sale lastimado.

Juan and Alberto were arguing about which video to watch. Juan punched Alberto and gave him a black eye. Both boys were forbidden to watch television for a week. The problem wasn't solved. Fighting only made it worse.

Juan y Alberto estaban discutiendo sobre qué video iban a ver. Juan le pegó a Alberto y le puso un ojo morado. Ambos fueron castigados sin ver televisión por una semana. El problema no fue resuelto. Pelear solo empeoró las cosas.

When you don't agree with someone, it's good to let that person know how you feel. Stay calm and listen. Take turns talking. This allows you to understand each other and to solve the problem without turning the discussion into a fight.

Cuando no estés de acuerdo con alguien, es bueno que le digas cómo te sientes. Mantente tranquilo y escucha. Tomen turnos para hablar. Así podrán entenderse y resolver el problema sin necesidad de pelear.

When you feel like fighting with someone, the first thing to do is calm down. Fighting will only make the situation worse. Both of you will be more upset and, even worse, both of you could get hurt. And the problem will not be fixed.

Cuando sientas ganas de pelear con alguien, lo primero que tienes que hacer es tranquilizarte. Pelear empeorará cualquier situación. Ambos estarán más enojados y, aun peor, ambos podrían lastimarse. Además, el problema no se resolverá.

Carla and her brother, David, were arguing. Carla was so angry that she wanted to punch him. But Carla knew that if she and David fought that they both would end up hurt. They agreed to to talk about the problem instead.

Carla y su hermano David estaban discutiendo. Carla estaba tan enojada que le quería pegar a David. Pero Carla sabía que en una pelea los dos acabarían lastimados. En lugar de pelear, ambos decidieron hablar del problema.

Whenever you have a problem with someone, the best thing to do is to talk it out. Each of you should try to see the other's side of things. The best way to resolve a **conflict** is to talk it out, not fight it out.

Siempre que tengas un problema con alguien, lo mejor que puedes hacer es platicarlo. Cada uno deberá tratar de ver la opinión del otro sobre el problema. La mejor manera de resolver un **conflicto** es hablar, no pelear.

Sometimes when you have a conflict with someone, you need to **compromise**. This means that both sides give up a little bit of what they want so that the conflict can be resolved.

Algunas veces, cuando tienes un conflicto con alguien, tienes que **llegar a un acuerdo**. Esto significa que ambas partes cederán un poco sobre lo que quieren para que se pueda resolver el problema.

Tina let her friend, Ana, borrow her bike. Ana, accidentally broke one of the pedals. They talked about the problem. Ana, agreed to replace the broken pedal. Tina thought that was fair. By compromising, the conflict was resolved.

Tina le prestó a su amiga Ana su bicicleta. Accidentalmente, Ana rompió uno de los pedales. Las amigas hablaron del problema. Ana aceptó comprar un pedal nuevo. Tina pensó que eso era lo justo. Llegando a un acuerdo se resolvió el conflicto.

Glossary

argument (AR-gyu-ment) Talking with someone about something you both disagree on.

compromise (KOM-pro-mize) Settling an argument by giving in a little.

conflict (KON-flikt) When two people see things differently.

physical (FIZ-zi-cal) Having to do with your body.

verbal (VER-bul) Using words.

Glosario

conflicto (el) Cuando dos personas ven algo de forma diferente.

discusión (la) Hablar con alguien sobre algo en lo que no estás de acuerdo.

físico(a) Relativo al cuerpo.

llegar a un acuerdo Cuando dos personas solucionan un problema cediendo un poco.

Index

Índice